How to Play the
Recorder

A step-by-step guide

Lisete da Silva

DK | Penguin Random House

Project editor Sam Priddy
Project art editor Fiona Macdonald
Managing editor Laura Gilbert
Managing art editor Diane Peyton Jones
Pre-production producer Ben Marcus
Producer Christine Ni
Jacket designer Lucy Sims
Publisher Sarah Larter
Publishing director Sophie Mitchell

Commissioned photography Andy Crawford

First published in Great Britain in 2015 by
Dorling Kindersley Limited
80 Strand, London, WC2R 0RL

Copyright © 2015 Dorling Kindersley Limited
A Penguin Random House Company
10 9 8 7 6 5 4 3 2 1
001–187497–Jul/2015

A CIP catalogue record for this book is
available from the British Library.
ISBN: 978-0-2411-9617-5

Printed and bound in China.

A WORLD OF IDEAS:
SEE ALL THERE IS TO KNOW

Contents

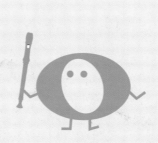

About the author

Lisete da Silva trained at the Royal Academy of Music in London, and has played with leading chamber groups and orchestras across Europe and South America. She has spent the last 20 years teaching the recorder and raising awareness of its historical and contemporary importance.

Special thanks to Mollenhauer for providing all of the recorders used in this book.

Introduction

Welcome to the wonderful world of recorders! They are a perfect first instrument to learn, and work as a great introduction to music in general.

This book will teach you everything you need to know to start playing a descant recorder. This is the most common type of recorder, and the easiest to play.

The exercises and tunes in this book have been designed to help you learn the art of the recorder. By the end, you will be able to play all sorts of fun pieces of music!

How the book works

There are two different types of pages. The coloured pages teach you how to play notes, while the others teach you everything else you need to know to play the recorder well.

You'll be playing music in no time!

Discover which holes you need to cover to play each note

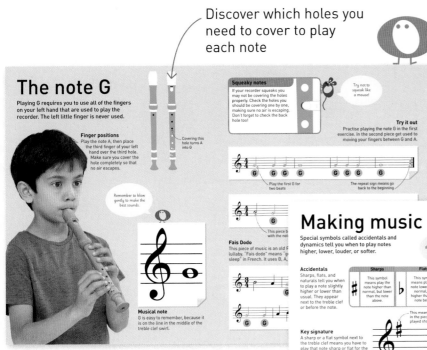

Simple explanations break everything down into easy chunks

Notes

Learn how to identify and play different notes, and then practise them with special exercises.

Music basics

Learn key skills that will help to make you a better recorder player.

Exercises give you a chance to practise what you've learnt

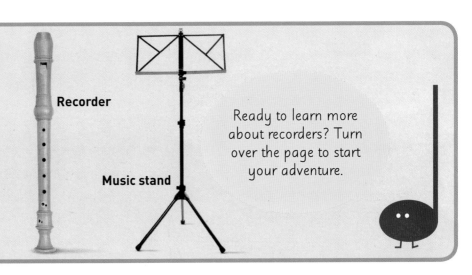

What you'll need

All you need for this book is a descant recorder. They can be found in most music shops. A music stand would also be useful for performing pieces, but this isn't essential, so don't worry if you haven't got one.

Recorder

Music stand

Ready to learn more about recorders? Turn over the page to start your adventure.

Your recorder

Before you start playing the recorder it's good to know what the different parts of it are called. It's also important to know where each one of your fingers goes.

Parts of a recorder

Recorders are usually made up of three parts that are gently screwed together. These parts are called the head section, the middle section, and the foot section.

This descant recorder is made out of wood, but they can be made from plastic.

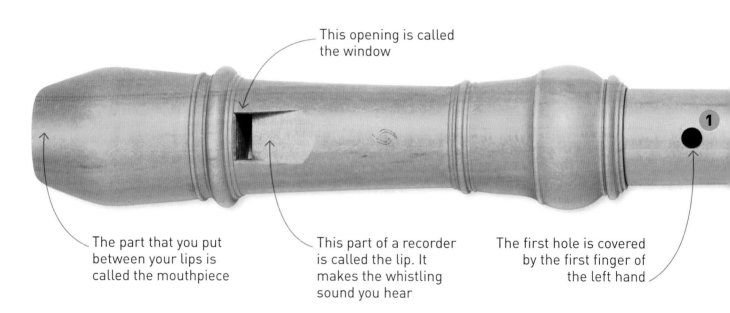

This opening is called the window

The part that you put between your lips is called the mouthpiece

This part of a recorder is called the lip. It makes the whistling sound you hear

The first hole is covered by the first finger of the left hand

Back view

There is only one hole on the back of a recorder. It is covered with the left thumb.

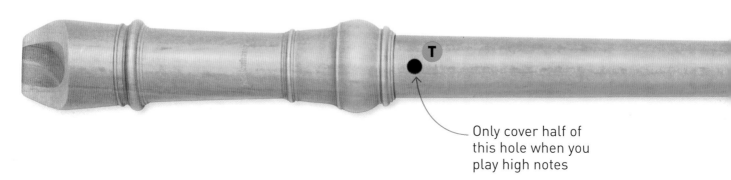

Only cover half of this hole when you play high notes

6

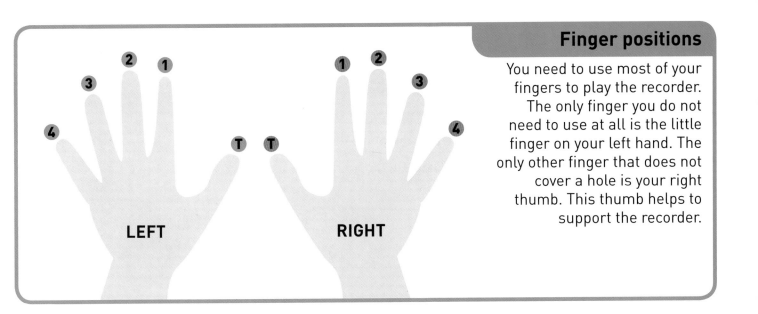

Finger positions

You need to use most of your fingers to play the recorder. The only finger you do not need to use at all is the little finger on your left hand. The only other finger that does not cover a hole is your right thumb. This thumb helps to support the recorder.

FOOT SECTION

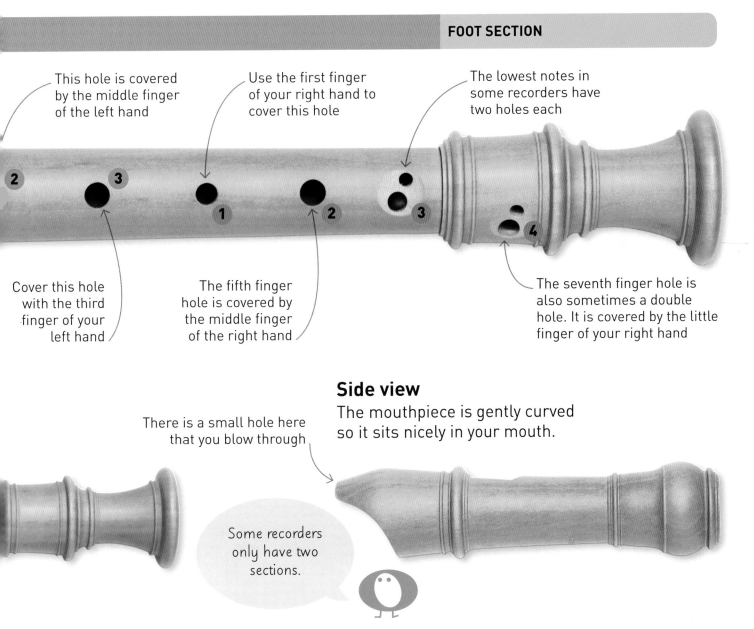

This hole is covered by the middle finger of the left hand

Use the first finger of your right hand to cover this hole

The lowest notes in some recorders have two holes each

Cover this hole with the third finger of your left hand

The fifth finger hole is covered by the middle finger of the right hand

The seventh finger hole is also sometimes a double hole. It is covered by the little finger of your right hand

Side view
The mouthpiece is gently curved so it sits nicely in your mouth.

There is a small hole here that you blow through

Some recorders only have two sections.

Recorder family

The recorder is one of the most popular instruments in the world. It is played by millions of people! Would you like to meet the family?

Types of recorder

The recorder family is one of the biggest instrument families. There are ten different sizes. The bigger they get, the lower the sound they make.

The biggest recorder ever made was as tall as a giraffe!

With big recorders, special keys help to cover the holes the player can't reach

Bass

Great bass

Timeline

Did you know the recorder is one of the oldest instruments in the world? It has been played ever since cave people were around.

Cave people
Prehistoric people made recorders out of bits of bone.

Henry VIII
While he was King of England, Henry VIII owned 76 recorders!

Shakespeare
Recorders appeared in William Shakespeare's play *Hamlet*.

18th century
People started listening to orchestras more, so the recorder became less popular.

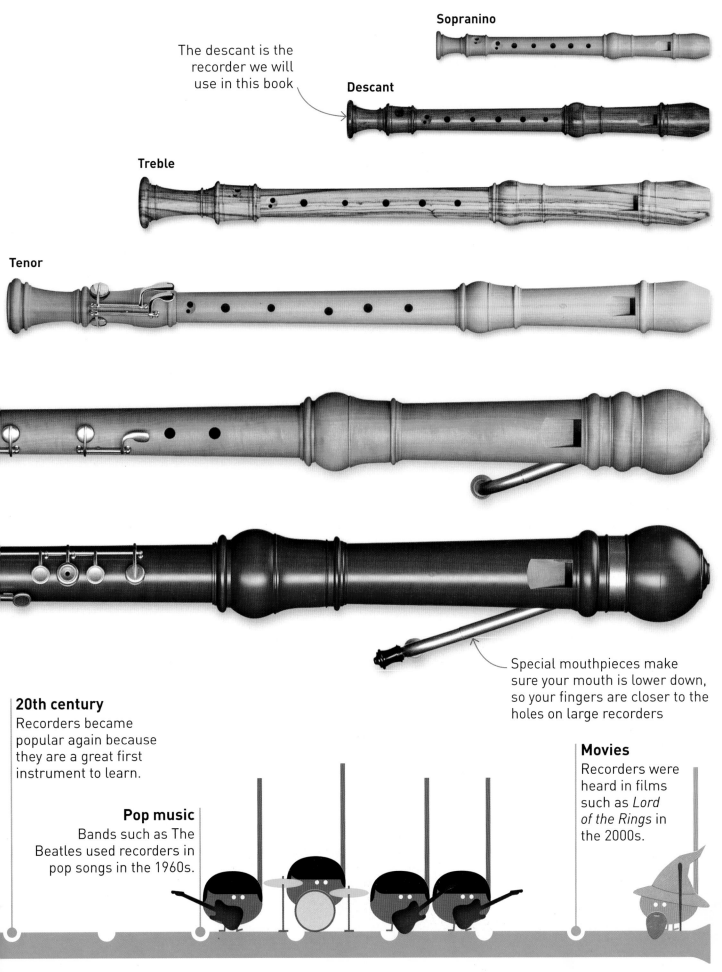

Sopranino

The descant is the recorder we will use in this book

Descant

Treble

Tenor

Special mouthpieces make sure your mouth is lower down, so your fingers are closer to the holes on large recorders

20th century
Recorders became popular again because they are a great first instrument to learn.

Pop music
Bands such as The Beatles used recorders in pop songs in the 1960s.

Movies
Recorders were heard in films such as *Lord of the Rings* in the 2000s.

Starting to play

It's time to start playing the recorder. First you need to learn how to blow into the recorder properly. This will help make the best sounds.

How to blow properly

Raise your hand up to your face and blow into your palm, trying to keep a steady stream of air. This is how you need to blow when playing your recorder.

Try to imagine you are blowing bubbles.

Your breath should go in a straight line in front of you

Making sound

Now you have got used to blowing, it's time to pick up your recorder and start making a noise. Follow these steps to see how a recorder makes a sound.

Don't blow too hard into your recorder, else it will squeak!

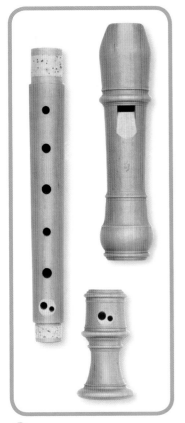

1 **Take your recorder apart**
Gently unscrew your recorder, being careful not to damage it.

2 **Blow gently**
Place the head section between your lips. Blow gently and see how long you can make a sound for. Your teeth and tongue should never touch the recorder.

3 **Cover the window**
The little window on the top of the recorder is what makes the noise. Cover it up with your fingers and try blowing. No sound will come out!

Looking after your recorder

It's important to clean your recorder every time you have finished using it. Special cleaning tools help to remove spit. A padded case protects the recorder when it is not in use.

Cleaning rod

Cleaning mop

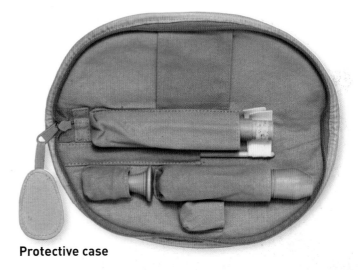
Protective case

Reading music

Written music tells you which notes to play on the recorder. It tells you how high or low they should sound, and how long they should be played for.

The stave

Music is written on a stave. It has five lines and four spaces. Each line and space has a note living in it.

A way of remembering the notes on the lines is "Every Good Bee Deserves Flowers".

This E (high E) sounds higher than the E at the bottom (low E)

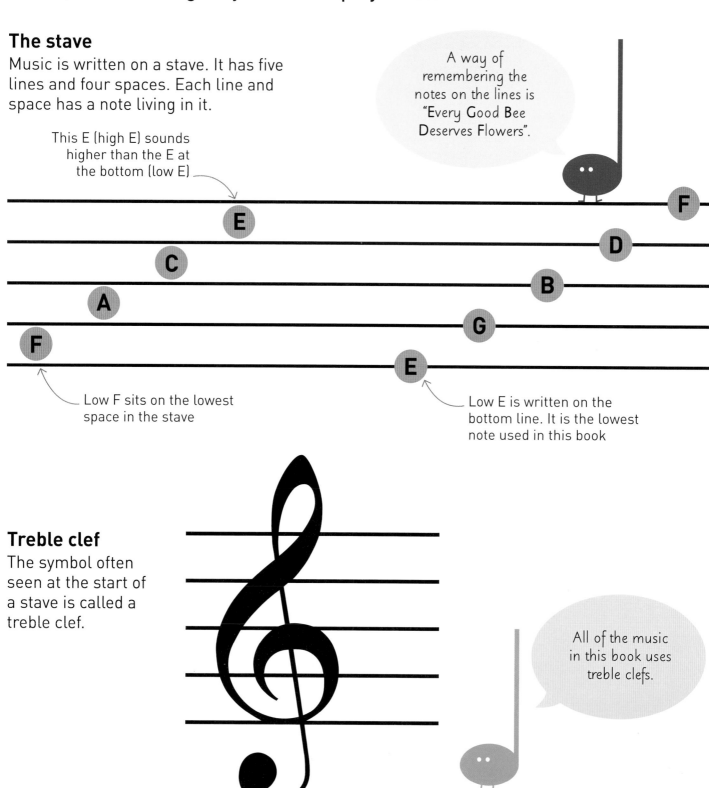

Low F sits on the lowest space in the stave

Low E is written on the bottom line. It is the lowest note used in this book

Treble clef

The symbol often seen at the start of a stave is called a treble clef.

All of the music in this book uses treble clefs.

Types of notes

Different types of notes show how long they should be played for. Music is counted in something called beats. Most of the music in this book is counted in crotchet beats.

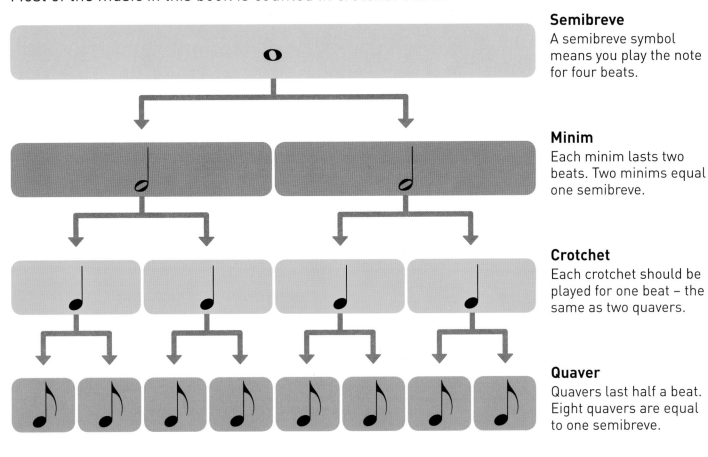

Semibreve
A semibreve symbol means you play the note for four beats.

Minim
Each minim lasts two beats. Two minims equal one semibreve.

Crotchet
Each crotchet should be played for one beat – the same as two quavers.

Quaver
Quavers last half a beat. Eight quavers are equal to one semibreve.

Dotted notes

A dotted note means you play the note, then play it for half as much again in the same breath.

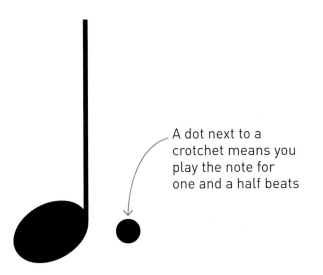

A dot next to a crotchet means you play the note for one and a half beats

Rests

A rest is a silence in music. If you see one, you stop and count in silence for the length of the rest.

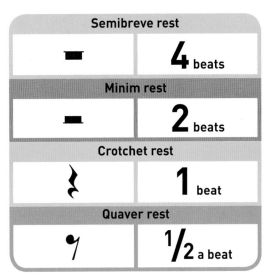

Semibreve rest	
▬	**4** beats
Minim rest	
▬	**2** beats
Crotchet rest	
𝄽	**1** beat
Quaver rest	
𝄾	**¹/₂** a beat

Time signatures

Music is divided up into bars. The two numbers next to the treble clef tell you how many beats are in a bar. This is called the time signature.

What does it mean?

A time signature tells you that each bar will have the same number of beats in it. It also lets you know what kind of beats they are.

Time signatures come after the treble clef

The top number tells you how many beats there are in each bar

The bottom number lets you know what kind of beats they are. The number 4 means the beats are crotchets

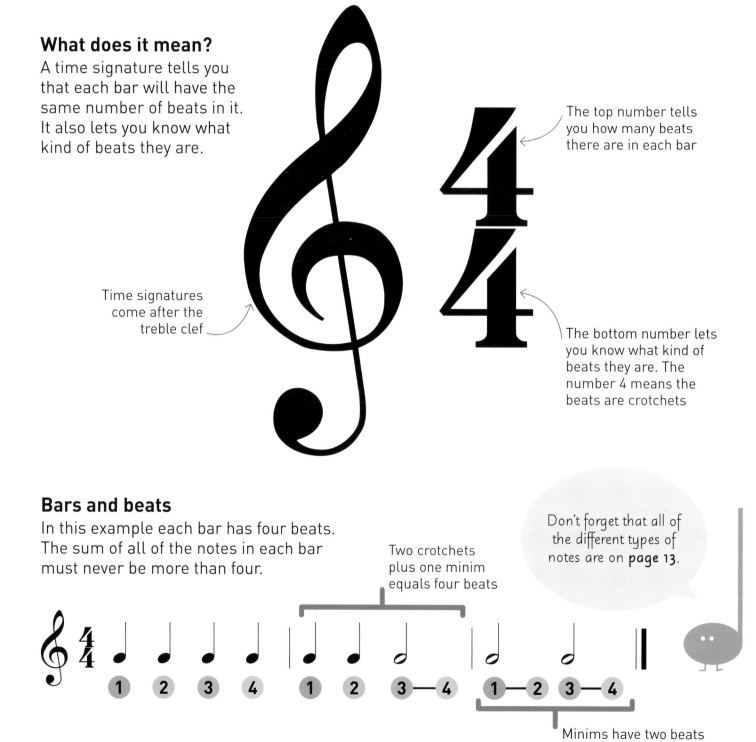

Bars and beats

In this example each bar has four beats. The sum of all of the notes in each bar must never be more than four.

Two crotchets plus one minim equals four beats

Don't forget that all of the different types of notes are on **page 13**.

Minims have two beats each, so two minims equal four beats

Clapping exercises

A good way to learn different time signatures is to clap along to the beats. These exercises introduce you to the other time signatures in the book.

For each note clap and wait for the correct number of beats!

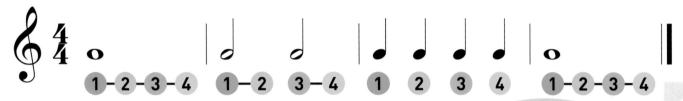

4/4 time signature

Each bar is worth four beats. Hold each note for the number of beats below it.

Two or more quavers next to each other are joined together like this.

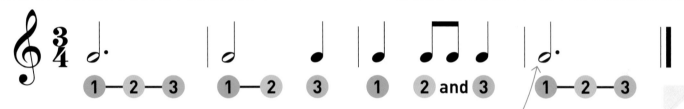

3/4 time signature

There are three crotchet beats in each bar in this time signature.

A dotted minim lasts for three beats

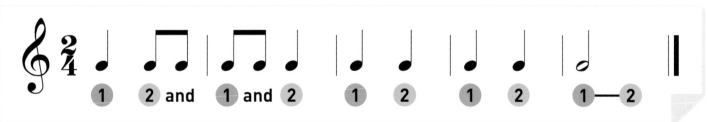

2/4 time signature

When you see a 2/4 time signature it means that there are only two crotchet beats in each bar.

Each bar in this time signature is worth three quaver beats

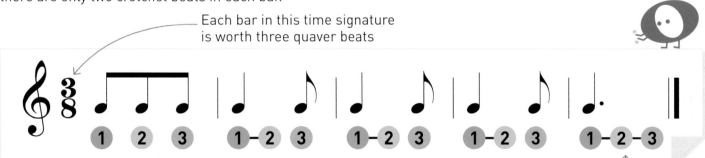

3/8 time signature

An eight at the bottom of a time signature means you count the bar in quaver beats. A quaver is worth half a crotchet.

A dotted crotchet lasts for three quaver beats

Breathing

Normally you don't think about breathing. However, to play the recorder you have to breathe in a special way. You can do this using a muscle in your stomach.

Use your muscles
When using your stomach muscles to breathe, it helps to imagine that it is like a balloon.

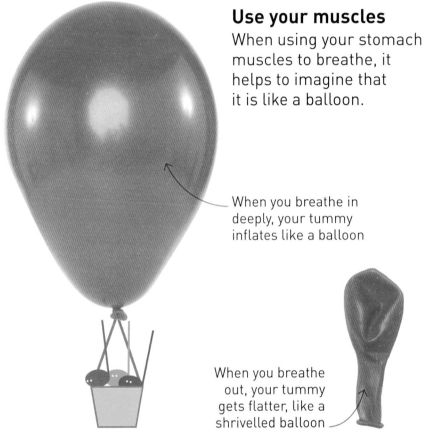

When you breathe in deeply, your tummy inflates like a balloon

When you breathe out, your tummy gets flatter, like a shrivelled balloon

How it works
Your stomach has a muscle called a diaphragm. It moves up and down to control the amount of air in your lungs.

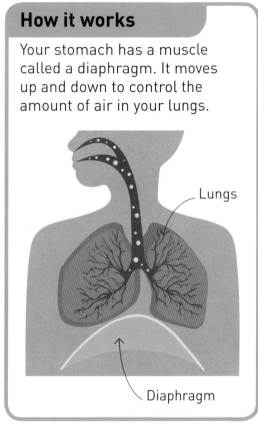

Lungs

Diaphragm

Good posture
Take a deep breath. Did your shoulders move? They shouldn't have! Try to breathe using just your stomach. This will help you blow into the recorder for longer.

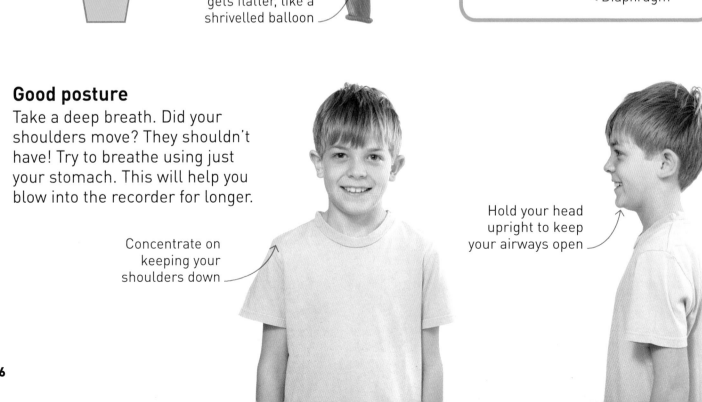

Concentrate on keeping your shoulders down

Hold your head upright to keep your airways open

Practise your breathing

Lie on your back and take a deep breath. Notice how your stomach rises and then falls. Now put a book on your stomach and practise moving the book up and down.

See how high you can move the book in the air!

Breathe out

Try using your stomach muscles to blow a steady stream of air. Breathe in through your mouth (filling up the balloon), then blow out hissing through your teeth. See how long you can keep it going!

SSSSSSSSSSSSSSSSSS

Make a hissing sound

You could also imagine you are filling a glass of water when you breathe in. Remember water hits the bottom of the glass first!

Tonguing

To produce sound you blow into a recorder, but to start each different note clearly you have to use your tongue. This is called tonguing.

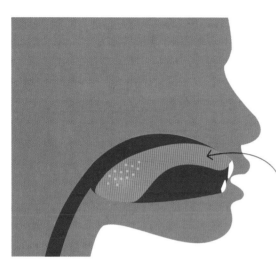

How to use your tongue
With your mouth almost closed, say the word "teddy". Notice how your tongue touches the inside of your mouth just above your top teeth.

Your tongue should touch the top of your teeth when blowing each note

When blowing normally you don't use your tongue, but with the recorder you need to!

Making the right sound
Put your hand in front of your lips and tongue a few times, saying the words "do, do, do". Notice the gentle burst of air on your hand each time.

Tongue the words gently

Your tongue should never touch the recorder, and neither should your teeth.

Practice exercises

Have a go at these tonguing exercises using the head section of your recorder. Remember to count out each note properly as you play it.

If you've forgotten how long each note lasts, turn back to **page 13**.

This time signature means there are four crotchet beats in each bar

A semibreve is four beats long

Minims last for two beats

Each bar lasts for two crotchet beats

Remember to tongue each note individually

Each bar is three crotchet beats long

This dotted note is three beats long

Hand positions

It is important to hold the recorder properly.
Certain fingers always cover the same holes,
so your hands are always in the same place.

Getting the basics right

The following steps will get you ready
to play your very first note. Follow
them carefully, and if you get stuck
just start again.

Make sure you
never grip your
recorder too hard.

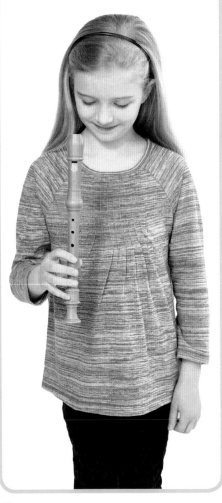

1 Pick up your recorder
With your left hand, hold the top of
your recorder in front of you. You
should be facing the hole at the back.

2 Start covering the holes
Bring your right hand up, adding
one finger at a time to the bottom
half of the recorder.

3 Position your thumb
Look to see where your right thumb
goes. It should be roughly level with
your first and second fingers.

4 Bring to your lips

Stand straight and look directly ahead. Then, bring the recorder to your lips. Make sure your head does not move towards the recorder.

5 Get your balance

Remove the first three fingers of your right hand. You will get "the three points of balance": lower lip, right thumb, and right little finger.

Balance the recorder on your lower lip

Your right little finger should still be touching the recorder

Rest the lower part of the recorder on your right thumb

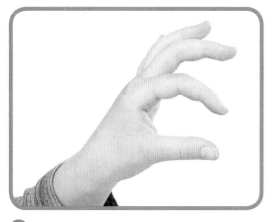

6 Introduce your left hand

To get ready to play your first note, make this shape with the thumb and first finger of your left hand.

7 Play your first note

Put your left thumb on the hole on the back of the recorder, and your finger on the first hole. Now blow your first note!

Now you've learnt the basics it's time to learn to read music!

The note B

The first note you are going to learn is B. It is the easiest note to play. You only need to cover two holes!

The holes you need to cover are coloured black

Only cover the first hole on the front of the recorder

Finger positions

Cover the first hole with the first finger on your left hand. The hole at the back should be covered completely by your left thumb. Now, gently blow into your recorder.

Remember to start each note by blowing a gentle "do" sound.

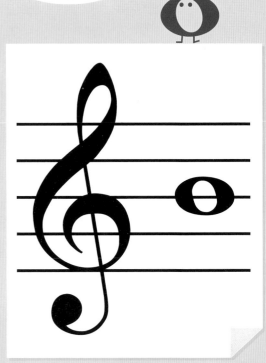

Musical note

The note B sits on the middle line of the stave.

Expert tip

A good way to remember how to play B is to touch your left thumb and first finger together. This is the shape you need to make when playing the note B.

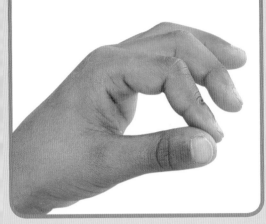

Are you ready to play your first bit of music?

Try it out

These pieces of music only have one note – B! Count the length of each note before you start so that you get the timings right.

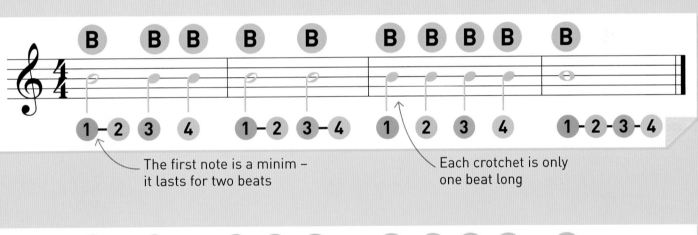

The first note is a minim – it lasts for two beats

Each crotchet is only one beat long

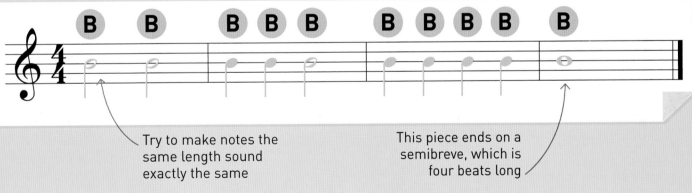

Try to make notes the same length sound exactly the same

This piece ends on a semibreve, which is four beats long

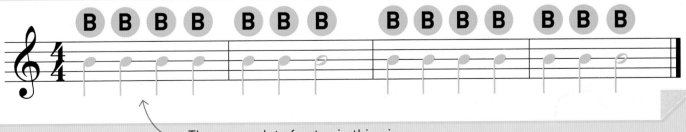

There are a lot of notes in this piece, so make sure you count carefully

The note A

The note below B is A. It is the second note you will learn, so you can now start to build your first tune.

Finger positions
Cover the first two holes with the first two fingers of your left hand. Cover the back hole with your left thumb.

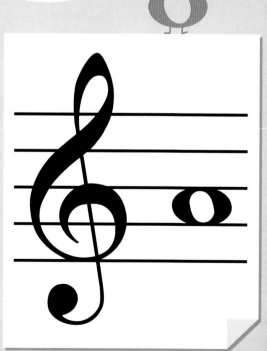

Covering this hole changes the note from B to A

Don't forget to breathe properly using your diaphragm.

Musical note
On a stave the note A is written below the note B. This means it will sound lower.

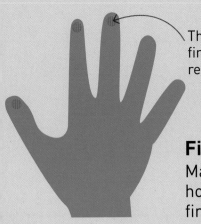

The pads of your fingers are coloured red here

Finger pads
Make sure you cover the holes with the pads of your fingers, not the tips or sides.

Don't raise your fingers too high when changing notes so you can change quickly.

Try it out
Now have a go playing a piece with the note A. Don't press too hard with your fingers.

The first note is four beats long

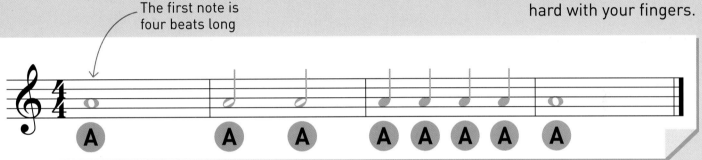

Play it on repeat
The double dots at the end of the line is a repeat sign. It means that once you finish the piece, you must play it again once more.

Keep your eyes peeled, as the repeat sign can be hard to spot!

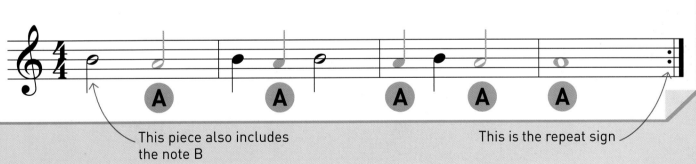

This piece also includes the note B

This is the repeat sign

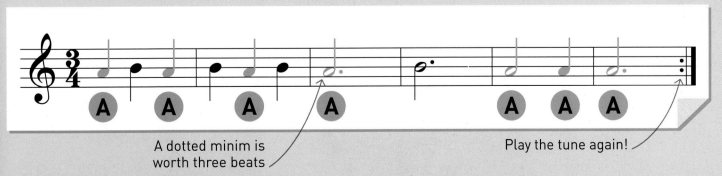

A dotted minim is worth three beats

Play the tune again!

The note G

Playing G requires you to use all of the fingers on your left hand that are used to play the recorder. The left little finger is never used.

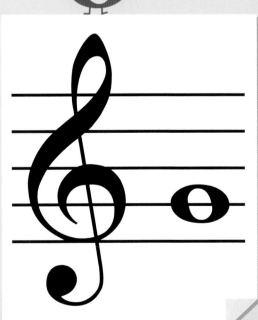

Finger positions

Play the note A, then place the third finger of your left hand over the third hole. Make sure you cover the hole completely so that no air escapes.

Covering this hole turns A into G

Remember to blow gently to make the best sounds.

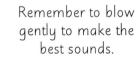

Musical note

G is easy to remember, because it is on the line in the middle of the treble clef swirl.

Squeaky notes

If your recorder squeaks you may not be covering the holes properly. Check the holes you should be covering one by one, making sure no air is escaping. Don't forget to check the back hole too!

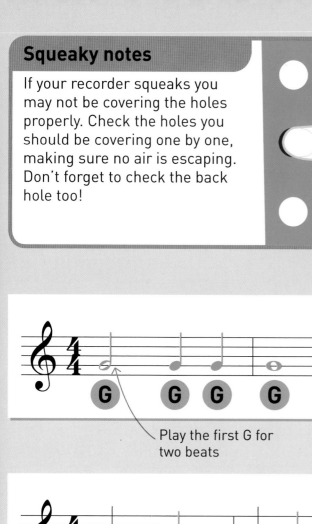

Try not to squeak like a mouse!

Try it out

Practise playing the note G in the first exercise. In the second piece get used to moving your fingers between G and A.

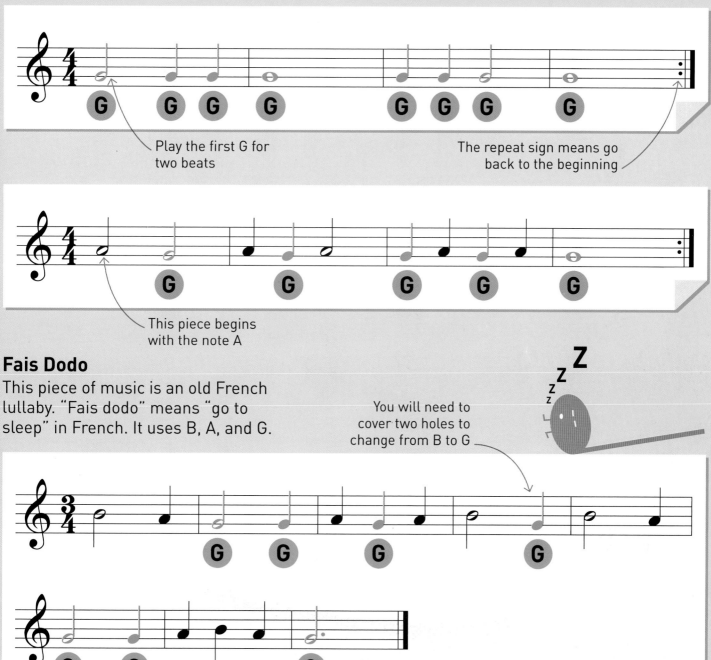

Play the first G for two beats

The repeat sign means go back to the beginning

This piece begins with the note A

Fais Dodo

This piece of music is an old French lullaby. "Fais dodo" means "go to sleep" in French. It uses B, A, and G.

You will need to cover two holes to change from B to G

Good technique

To play the recorder well it is important to stand up properly, and to know when to breathe. Most importantly, you must practise a lot!

Standing tall

When playing it is important to have a relaxed and straight back, keep your shoulders down, and look straight ahead. This helps you to breathe better.

GOOD vs **BAD**

Imagine there is a piece of string holding your head upright

Look straight in front of you

Keep your back upright

Your whole body should be relaxed, with no tension in your muscles

Lowering your head will change the way the recorder sounds

You must not bend your back

Don't bend your knees too much

Breath mark

While playing you must not forget to breathe! Breath marks written above the stave let you know when to do this.

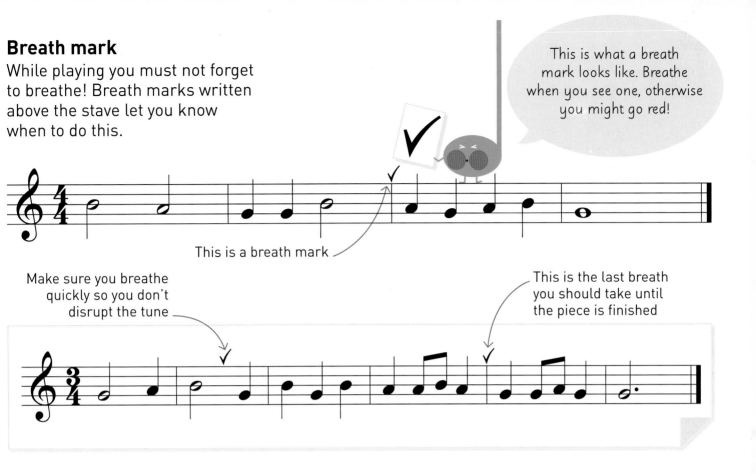

This is what a breath mark looks like. Breathe when you see one, otherwise you might go red!

This is a breath mark

Make sure you breathe quickly so you don't disrupt the tune

This is the last breath you should take until the piece is finished

Practising tips

To become a good musician you have to practise little and often. Here are two tunes for you to play. They use all of the notes you have learnt so far.

Always make sure you are counting the beats properly.

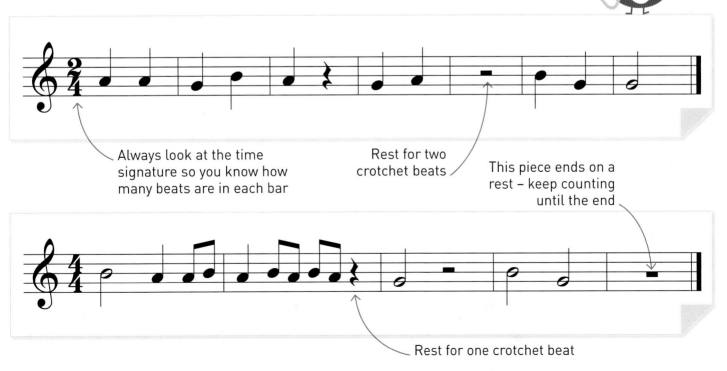

Always look at the time signature so you know how many beats are in each bar

Rest for two crotchet beats

This piece ends on a rest – keep counting until the end

Rest for one crotchet beat

High C

High C (also written as C') is the highest note in this book so far. There is another C, low C, that will appear later in the book.

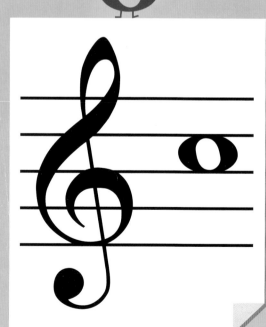

Cover the second hole

Finger positions

To play high C, first play A, then gently lift the first finger of your left hand off the first hole.

Don't forget to keep a straight back while playing the note.

Musical note

High C is written in the second space on the stave.

See-saw music

Use these practice tunes to see-saw between high C and A, and high C and B. The second piece is quite tricky.

See how long you can see-saw between A and high C in one breath.

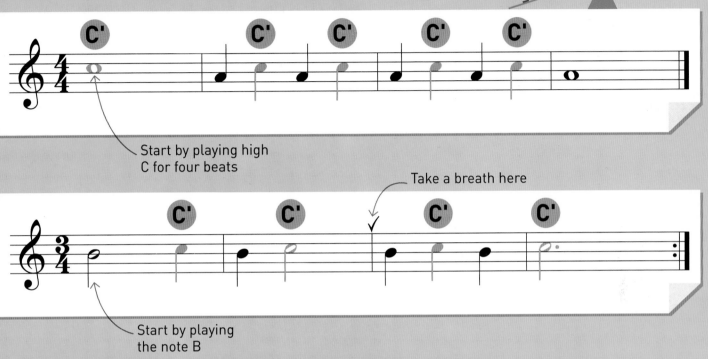

Start by playing high C for four beats

Take a breath here

Start by playing the note B

Try it out

Here are more exercises using high C for you to practise. Remember to breathe when you see the breath marks above the stave.

Don't forget to breathe when you see this mark

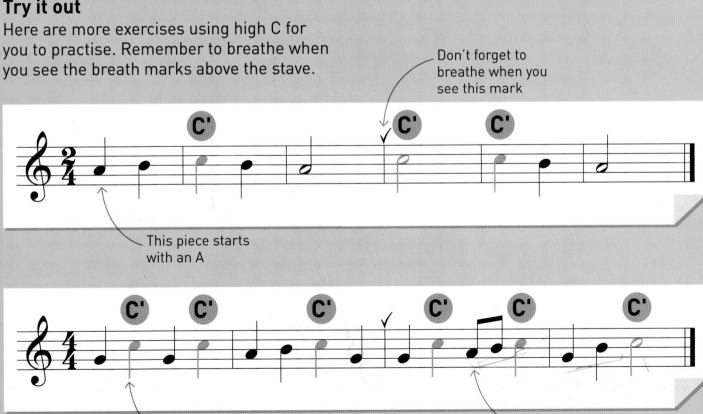

This piece starts with an A

You have to remove two fingers to go from a G to a high C

Each quaver is worth half a crotchet

High D

The note high D (also written as D') is special, because you only need one finger to play it. The back hole is uncovered, so keep the recorder supported with your right hand.

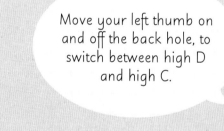

This is the first note in this book that has the back hole uncovered

Finger positions
Firstly play the note high C. Then move your left thumb away from the back hole. This is high D.

Move your left thumb on and off the back hole, to switch between high D and high C.

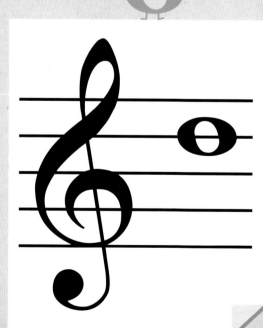

Musical note
High D is written on the second line of the stave.

Hand positions

When playing high D in a piece, always check where all of your other fingers are. If they are too high, you will waste time moving them down to play the next part of the tune. Keep them low and at the ready.

Good hand positions
Keep your fingers close to the holes. This will help you play the next note more smoothly.

Bad hand positions
If your fingers are too high it is harder to balance the recorder, and it takes longer to change notes.

Try it out

Practise these simple exercises using high D, high C, and B.

Place your thumb over the back hole to play high C

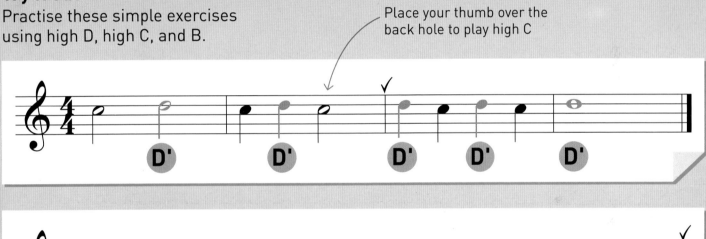

D' D' D' D' D'

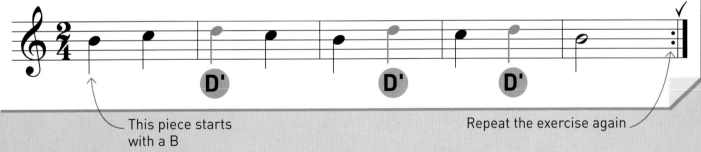

This piece starts with a B

Repeat the exercise again

D' D' D'

Dragon dance

This piece is more difficult – it uses every note you have learnt so far. It's a good idea to practise fingering each note before you start playing.

Remove two fingers and one thumb to change from G to high D

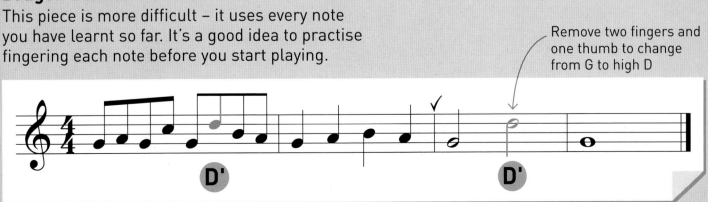

D' D'

Tied notes

Two or more of the same note can be tied
together to make one long note. This is useful
when playing notes that go over two bars.

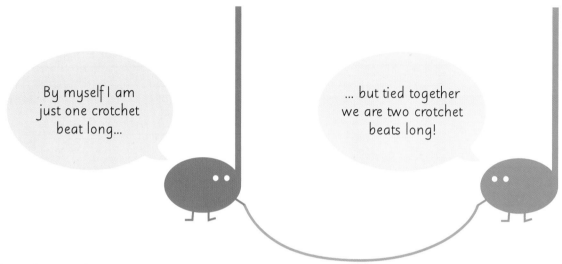

How it works

Play the first note and count the second,
but do not tongue the second note.

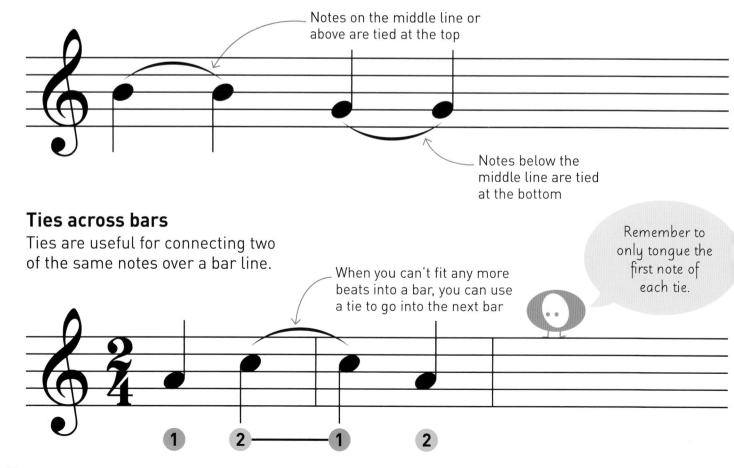

Ties across bars

Ties are useful for connecting two
of the same notes over a bar line.

Try it out

Practise playing tied notes with this tune. Add the beats up carefully when you play tied notes, and keep blowing until the end of the second note.

This tie is worth three crotchet beats

Play the last note for six crotchet beats

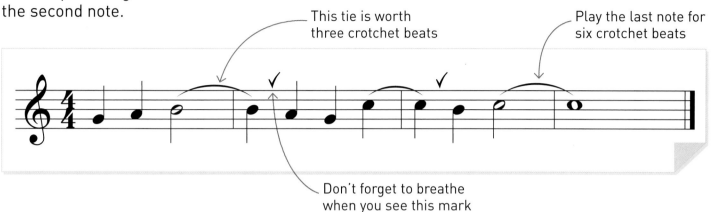

Don't forget to breathe when you see this mark

Tied up

Here is a longer piece of music that includes tied notes. Take a good breath before you start, and remember to breathe when you see the tick mark.

Play this note for three beats

This piece should be played smoothly.

This note needs to be played for six beats

Take a breath before the last big note

Long and short notes

To make a note longer, it can be joined to two or more notes in a slur. To make a note shorter, it can be played in a special style called staccato.

Slurred notes are joined by an arch, like tied notes, but unlike tied notes they connect different notes (for example B and C)

Slurred notes

A slur joins two or more different notes. They should be played as one long note, and only the first note should be tongued.

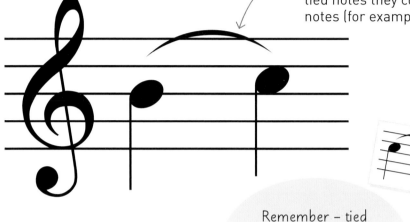

Remember – tied notes only join together notes on the same line.

Slurred note exercises

For each slur in these exercises, tongue the first note with a gentle "do". Then only tongue again once the slur arch is over.

This note should be played as part of the slur, but shouldn't be tongued

Tongue the first note of each slur

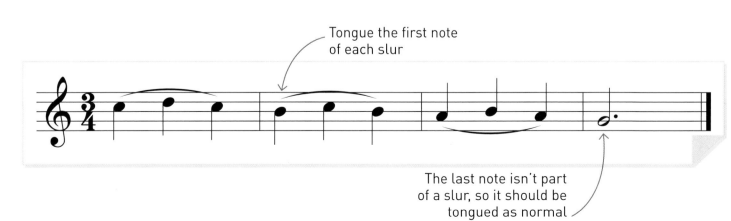

The last note isn't part of a slur, so it should be tongued as normal

Staccato notes

Staccato notes are short, punchy notes played with a quick movement of the tip of your tongue. To play a staccato note, finger the note like normal and tongue the words "ti, ti, ti".

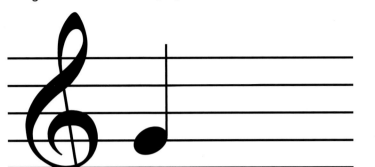

When playing staccato notes, imagine you are bouncing a ball. This is the kind of bouncy sound you need to make.

Staccato notes are written with a dot above or below the note

Staccato note exercises

When playing staccato notes, it is important that your tonguing movements are shorter than normal.

Don't confuse staccato notes with dotted notes (see **page 13**).

Don't forget to play the notes without dots smoothly

Each bar in this exercise is two crotchet beats long

These staccato notes are quavers

Practice tunes

These pieces of music bring together all of the notes you have learnt so far, as well as legato, staccato, and slurred notes.

Legato

Legato is the word for normal smooth notes. They are the opposite of staccato notes. Practise both of them in this piece of music.

Staccato notes will have a dot either above or below them

Up until now most of the notes you have played have been legato.

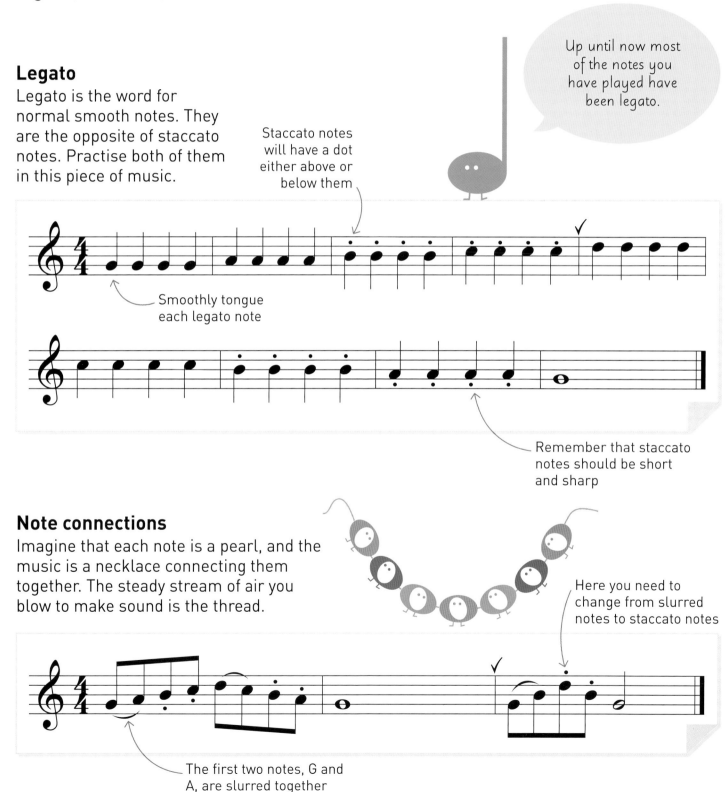

Smoothly tongue each legato note

Remember that staccato notes should be short and sharp

Note connections

Imagine that each note is a pearl, and the music is a necklace connecting them together. The steady stream of air you blow to make sound is the thread.

Here you need to change from slurred notes to staccato notes

The first two notes, G and A, are slurred together

Winter Goodbye

This piece is a traditional German tune celebrating the end of winter and the arrival of spring.

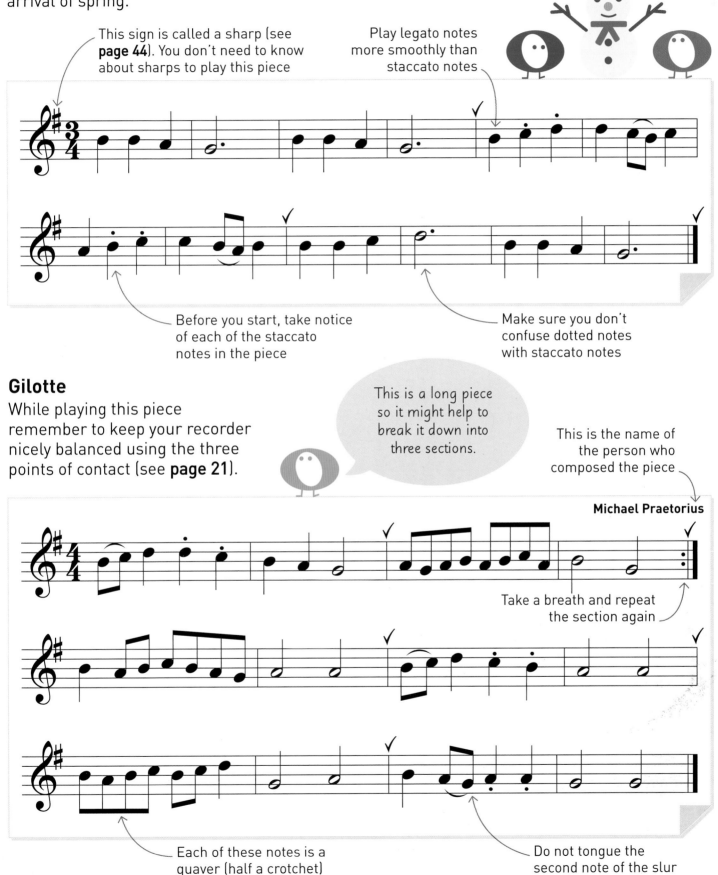

This sign is called a sharp (see **page 44**). You don't need to know about sharps to play this piece

Play legato notes more smoothly than staccato notes

Before you start, take notice of each of the staccato notes in the piece

Make sure you don't confuse dotted notes with staccato notes

Gilotte

While playing this piece remember to keep your recorder nicely balanced using the three points of contact (see **page 21**).

This is a long piece so it might help to break it down into three sections.

This is the name of the person who composed the piece

Michael Praetorius

Take a breath and repeat the section again

Each of these notes is a quaver (half a crotchet)

Do not tongue the second note of the slur

Low E

To play low E you need to use your right hand for the first time. This note will sound lower than the others you have played.

Finger positions

First play the note G (see **pages 26–27**). Now gently place the first two fingers of your right hand over the fourth and fifth holes.

The two double holes at the bottom remain uncovered

When adding lots of fingers to the recorder, take care that no air is escaping where it shouldn't be.

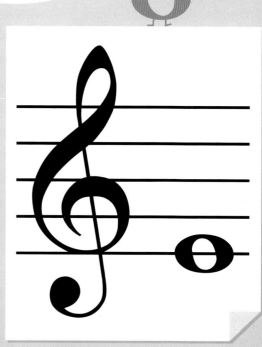

Musical note

Low E is written on the bottom line of the stave.

Try it out

Slur between G and low E in the first exercise, and then alternate between low E and a variety of higher notes in the second.

The first two fingers on your right hand should work as a team, moving up and down together.

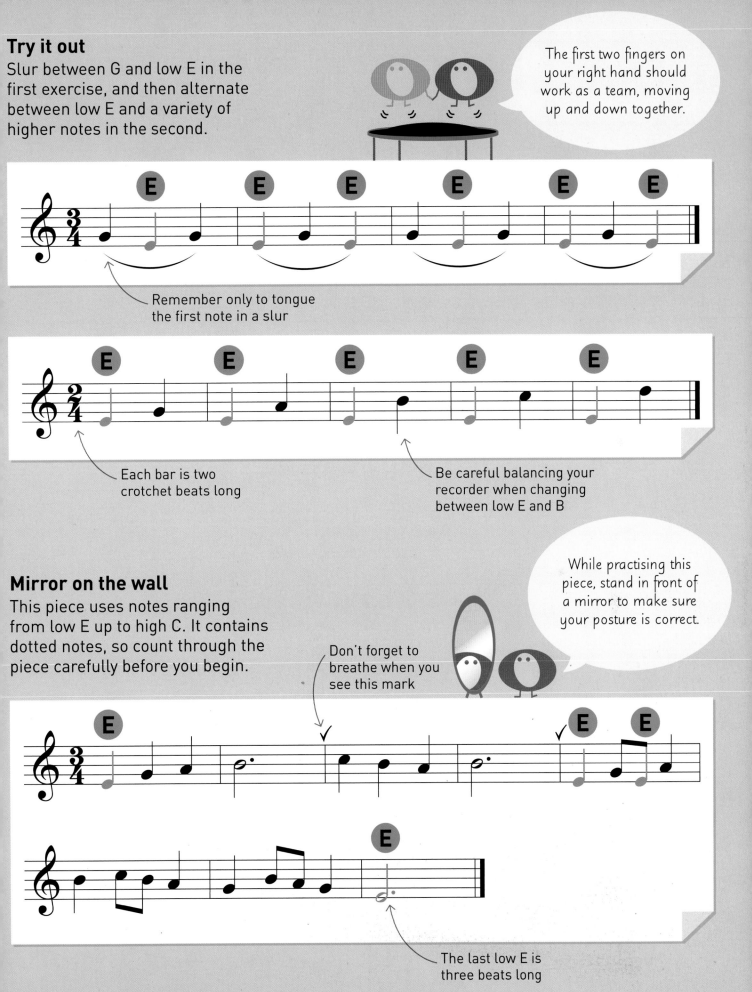

Remember only to tongue the first note in a slur

Each bar is two crotchet beats long

Be careful balancing your recorder when changing between low E and B

Mirror on the wall

This piece uses notes ranging from low E up to high C. It contains dotted notes, so count through the piece carefully before you begin.

While practising this piece, stand in front of a mirror to make sure your posture is correct.

Don't forget to breathe when you see this mark

The last low E is three beats long

Low D

Low D is a low note that should be played gently. To play it you have to cover the first double hole on the recorder for the first time.

Cover this double hole

Finger positions

Finger and play the note E. Notice how the third finger on your right hand hovers just above the first double hole. Place it down gently, making sure you cover both small holes completely.

Be patient with low D. If it squeaks a little, go back up to E or even G, and then come back down again.

Musical note

Low D is written on the space underneath the last line of the stave.

Escaping air

It is easy to make mistakes when covering a double hole. The most common problem is air escaping from the side. If it sounds funny, check that your third finger is covering both holes completely.

Can you feel both holes with your finger? If you can't then air might be escaping.

Try it out

Get used to the feel of playing low D with these two exercises. Pay particular attention to the double hole.

Go up and down with the third finger of your right hand, getting used to the finger movement

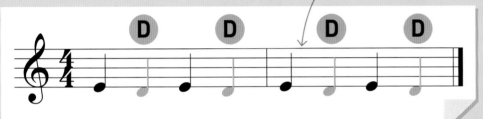

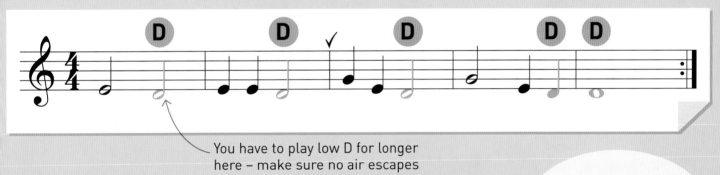

You have to play low D for longer here – make sure no air escapes

Hot Cross Buns

This tune is an old English nursery rhyme about sweet buns filled with raisins.

It's not a good idea to eat and play the recorder at the same time!

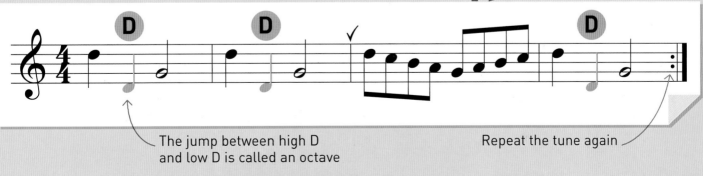

The jump between high D and low D is called an octave

Repeat the tune again

Making music

Special symbols called accidentals and dynamics tell you when to play notes higher, lower, louder, or softer.

Learn how to play the note F# (F sharp) on **pages 46-47**.

Accidentals

Sharps, flats, and naturals tell you when to play a note slightly higher or lower than usual. They appear next to the treble clef or before the note.

Sharps	Flats	Naturals
♯ This symbol means play the note higher than normal, but lower than the note above.	♭ This symbol means play the note lower than normal, but higher than the note below.	♮ This symbol means the note should be played as normal again.

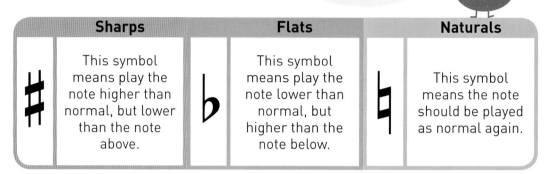

This means all F notes in the piece must be played sharp

All B notes must be played flat

Key signature

A sharp or a flat symbol next to the treble clef means you have to play that note sharp or flat for the whole piece. This is called the key signature.

This F should be played normally

This F should be played sharp

Before a note

A sharp or flat written in front of a note means you play that note sharp or flat for the rest of the bar, unless a natural appears.

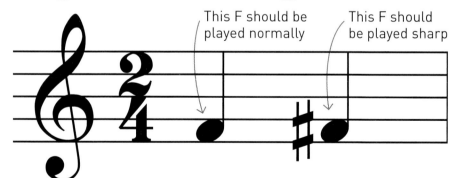

This means play all F notes in the bar as F sharp

Naturals

Naturals also appear in front of the note, and reverse the effects of any sharps or flats earlier in the piece.

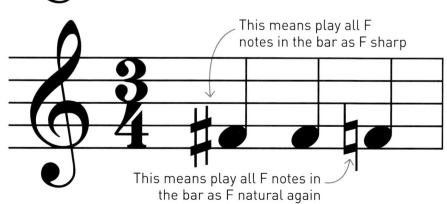

This means play all F notes in the bar as F natural again

Loud and quiet

These symbols are called dynamics. They tell you when to play notes loudly or quietly. If you see a dynamic, it means that all of the following notes should be played in that style, until you see another dynamic.

To play a note loudly, you blow harder. To play a note quietly, blow gently.

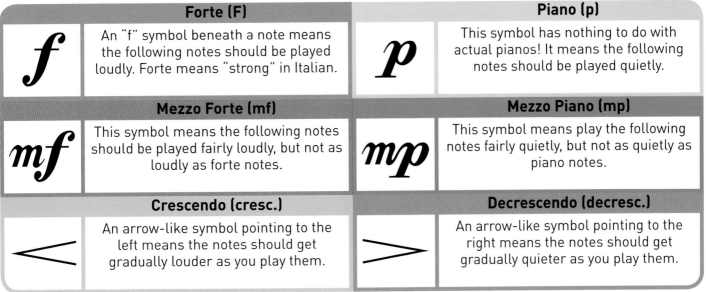

Forte (F)		Piano (p)	
f	An "f" symbol beneath a note means the following notes should be played loudly. Forte means "strong" in Italian.	*p*	This symbol has nothing to do with actual pianos! It means the following notes should be played quietly.
Mezzo Forte (mf)		**Mezzo Piano (mp)**	
mf	This symbol means the following notes should be played fairly loudly, but not as loudly as forte notes.	*mp*	This symbol means play the following notes fairly quietly, but not as quietly as piano notes.
Crescendo (cresc.)		**Decrescendo (decresc.)**	
<	An arrow-like symbol pointing to the left means the notes should get gradually louder as you play them.	>	An arrow-like symbol pointing to the right means the notes should get gradually quieter as you play them.

Try it out

See how the same notes can sound different depending on how hard you blow. Play the notes B-A-G loudly, and then quietly.

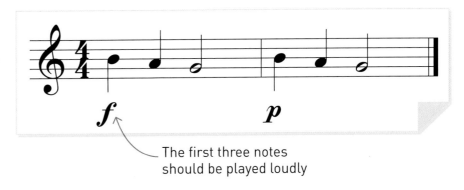

The first three notes should be played loudly

The Elephant and the Mouse

Before playing this piece look through it and take note of the different dynamics. The elephant should be loud, while the mouse should be quiet (but not squeaky!).

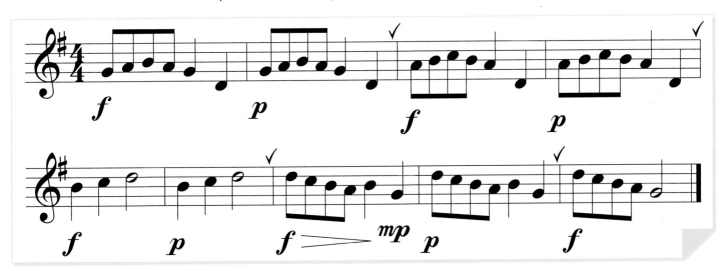

The note F#

F sharp (F#) is the first sharp note in this book. It sounds slightly higher than F, but slightly lower than G (the note above F).

Finger positions

Start by playing the note low D. Then lift the first finger on your right hand. This is F#.

Uncover this hole to turn low D into F#

Make sure any fingers not being used hover just above the holes.

Musical note

The note F# is written on the fourth space on the stave. It has a sharp symbol in front of it.

Dog hand-shape

It's helpful to remember that to play the note F#, you have to make the shape of a dog with your right hand. Your first and little fingers should be in the air, while your second and third fingers are down.

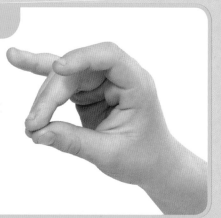

Try it out

Practise F# with these see-saw exercises. Don't forget to breathe when you see the breath mark.

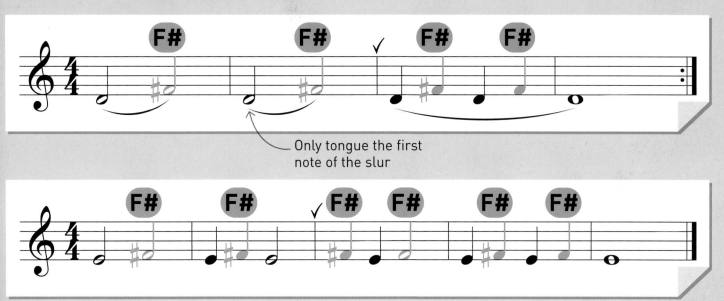

Only tongue the first note of the slur

Goddesses

This piece has a sharp symbol next to the treble clef on the top F note (there are two F notes on a stave). This means all F notes in the piece must be played sharp.

No one knows who wrote this piece!

Play these notes fairly loudly

ANON.

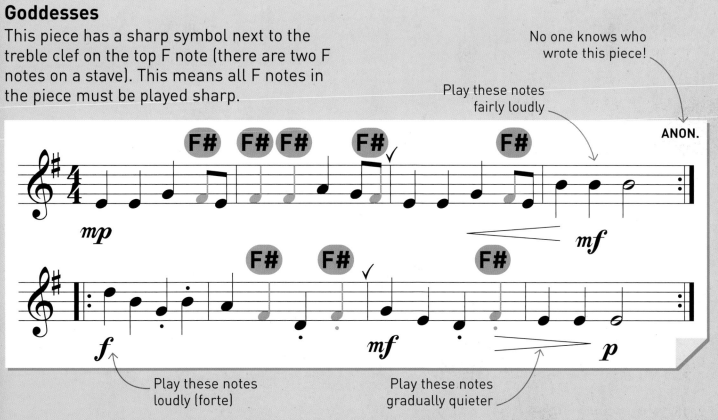

Play these notes loudly (forte)

Play these notes gradually quieter

Low C

This note is the lowest one you can play on your descant recorder. To play low C, you need to cover all of the holes.

Finger positions

First finger and play low D, and then place the little finger of your right hand on the last double hole. This is low C.

Cover both holes with your right little finger

Because all of the holes need to be covered to play this note, take special care that no air escapes.

Musical note

Low C is written on a special line beneath the stave. This is called a ledger line.

Foot section

Before you start playing, look at the position of the last double hole of the recorder. Most recorders have a movable foot joint, which can be adjusted. It should be rotated slightly to the right of the other holes, so your little finger can cover it easily.

Try it out

Pay attention to how your fingers lie on the holes, making sure you're using the pads to cover them.

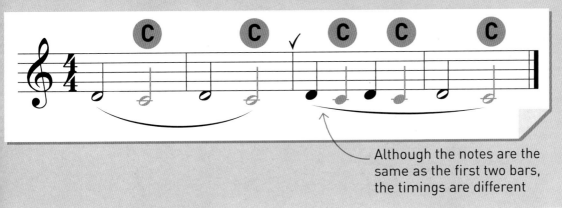

Although the notes are the same as the first two bars, the timings are different

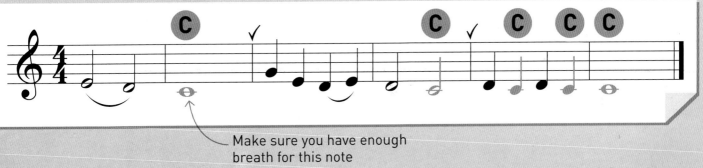

Make sure you have enough breath for this note

Morning Mood

This Norwegian piece of music is about the rising of the sun. It is a low piece – the highest note is an A.

Edvard Grieg

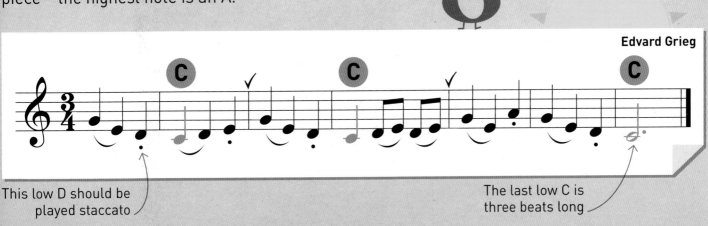

This low D should be played staccato

The last low C is three beats long

F natural

This note is the natural version of F#. Once you have learnt it you will be able to play your first scale – the C major scale (see **page 52**).

Finger positions

First play low C, by covering all of the holes. Now gently lift the second finger of your right hand off its hole. This is F natural.

This is the only hole that should remain uncovered

This note sounds slightly lower than F#.

Musical note

The note F is written on the same line as F#, but doesn't have the sharp symbol written in front of it.

Try it out

Play between low C and F natural, slurring the notes. Then experiment changing between low E and F natural.

The second finger on your right hand doesn't have to lift very far to change from low C to F natural.

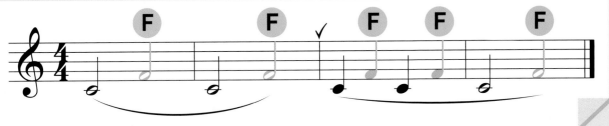

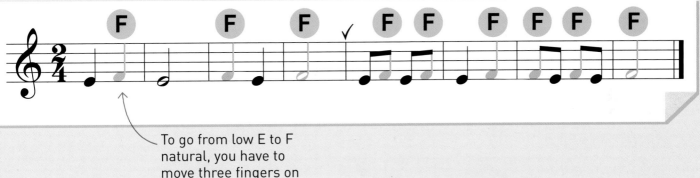

To go from low E to F natural, you have to move three fingers on your right hand

F hand position

The piece of music Midnight Stroll requires you to move down from a G to an F natural. Practise the F natural hand position to prepare. The second finger on your right hand should be raised, but all of the others should be down.

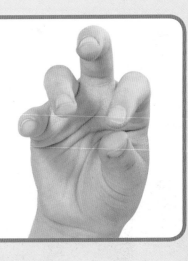

Midnight Stroll

When playing this piece remember your breath should bind the notes together, like the thread of a necklace.

Play the notes fairly softly

Only tongue the first note of the slur

Scales

A scale is eight notes, one after the other, getting higher or lower. Scales start and end on notes of the same letter.

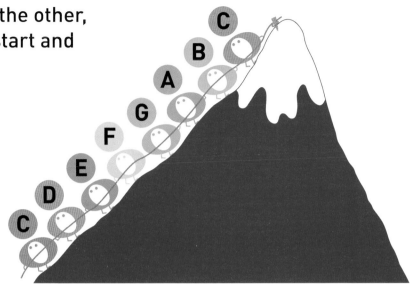

C Major scale

Your first scale is C Major. It uses all of the notes you have learnt so far, and has no sharps or flats.

C Major scale exercise

Practise changing between notes in this C Major scale exercise. Pay close attention to how your fingers move together, in particular from low E to F natural, and from F natural to G.

This is called an ascending scale

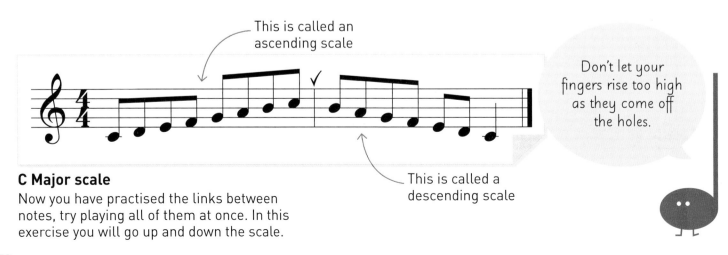

This is called a descending scale

Don't let your fingers rise too high as they come off the holes.

C Major scale

Now you have practised the links between notes, try playing all of them at once. In this exercise you will go up and down the scale.

High C#

To play the D Major scale, you need to know how to play high C sharp. Finger and play the note A, then gently remove your left thumb from the back hole.

The back hole should be open

Musical note

High C# is written on the same line as high C, but with a sharp symbol in front of it.

Try it out

See-saw between A and high C# to get used to the thumb movements.

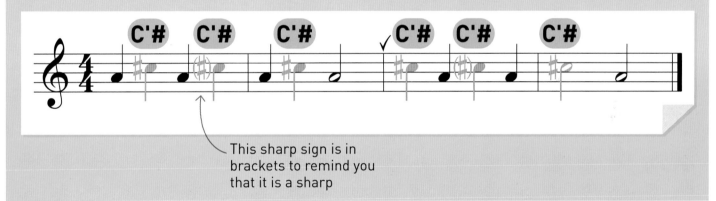

C'# C'# C'# C'# C'# C'#

This sharp sign is in brackets to remind you that it is a sharp

D Major scale

Play the D Major scale. See how fluid you can make the connections between the different notes.

Take a breath in between scales

It's good to practise scales regularly, so that you remember how to play all of the notes.

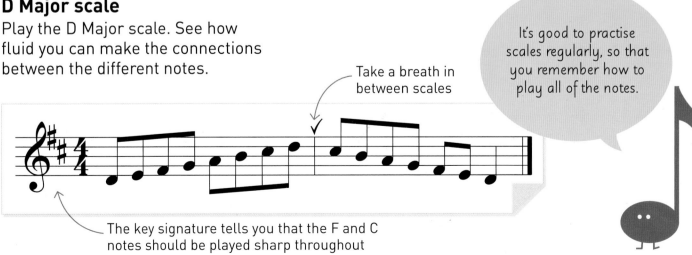

The key signature tells you that the F and C notes should be played sharp throughout

Duets

When you play a piece of music with another player,
it is called a duet. You must listen carefully to your
partner – keep in rhythm and don't play too loudly.

Double lines

Duets are written on
connected lines. The
first player plays the
top line, and the
second player plays
the bottom line.

One person plays
this line...

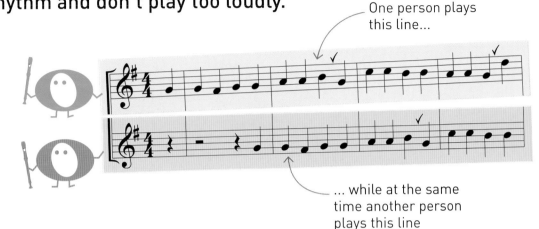

... while at the same
time another person
plays this line

Tallis's Canon

The key to playing a duet well is keeping
the beat. Count carefully – both players
should start and finish at the same time.

While the first person plays
an A, the second person
plays G (directly below it)

Thomas Tallis

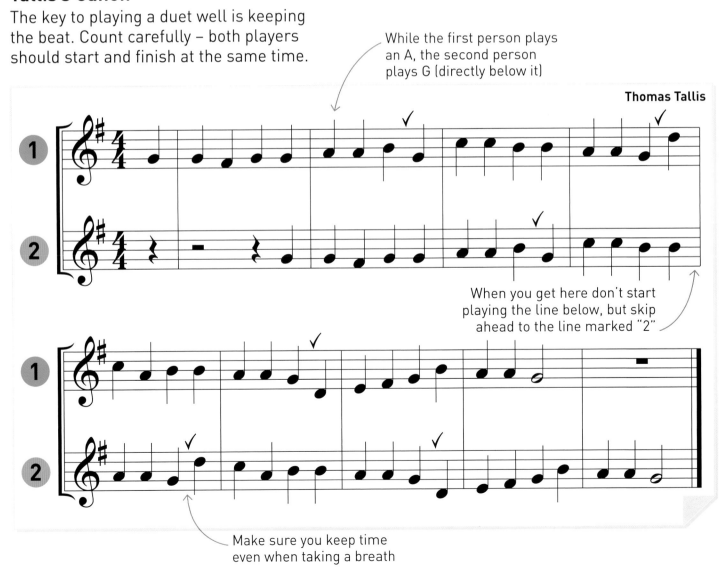

When you get here don't start
playing the line below, but skip
ahead to the line marked "2"

Make sure you keep time
even when taking a breath

Minuet

A minuet was a dance that was played at the court of a king or queen. It should be played gracefully and lightly.

Anon.

High E

This note is the highest in the book. To play high E you have to uncover half of the thumb hole. As you learn more notes in the future you'll do this a lot.

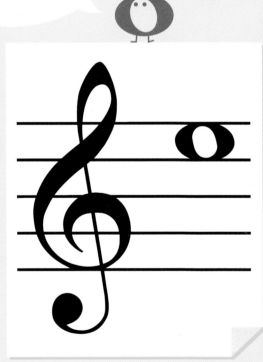

This hole should be half uncovered

Finger positions

First finger and play a low E. Now gently bend your left thumb so it uncovers half of the hole at the back. This is how you play high E.

High E sounds a bit like low E – it is just a higher version of the same note.

Musical note

The note high E is written on the first space in the stave.

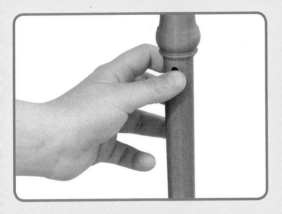

Bent thumb

Practise gently bending your thumb to uncover the right side of the back hole. Be careful not to lose balance of your recorder.

Feel the edge of the back hole with your thumb to make sure you are uncovering half of it.

Try it out

See-saw between low E and high E. You'll need to blow a little more to play high E.

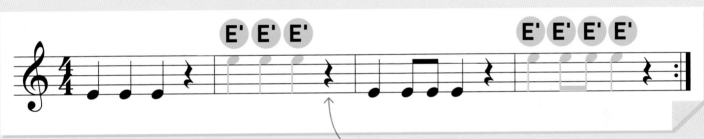

Use the rests to bend and straighten your thumb, ready for the next note

This means we think Rameau was the composer, but we are not sure!

Frère Jacques

This piece is a famous French nursery rhyme about someone sleeping too much!

Attributed to Jean-Philippe Rameau

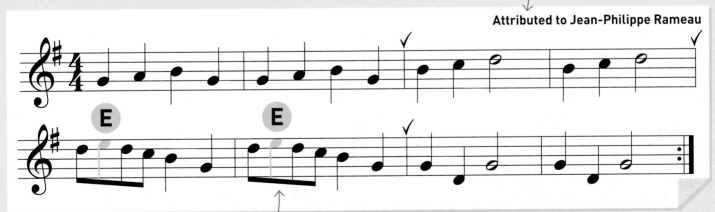

Take care to adjust your thumb correctly

Get practising

The key to becoming a better recorder player is practice. It's best to practise little and often.

Top tips

Before each practice session go through this checklist. It will help to make sure you are doing the basics correctly.

Checklist

☐ **Check your posture**

Stand in front of a mirror so you can see how you are holding the recorder. You should have a relaxed, straight posture.

Turn to **page 28** to see exactly how you should be standing.

☐ **Think about your breathing**

Breathe using your stomach muscles. Do not raise your shoulders, and blow out a steady stream of air.

Remember how your stomach inflates and deflates like a balloon (see **page 16**).

☐ **Keep your balance**

Make sure your recorder is balanced correctly using the three points of contact: lower lip, right thumb, and your right little finger (see **page 21**).

☐ **Look at the position of your fingers**

Keep your fingers hovering low above their holes so that they can be used quickly. This will help you to move your fingers more efficiently.

Don't forget to clean your recorder after playing.

☐ **Watch your mouth!**

Remember that your tongue should touch the top of your teeth, not the recorder. Your teeth should never touch the recorder either.

Exercise 1

Before you begin practising, play a couple of scales. This will help you to get a fluid movement between notes.

This is a D Major scale

Exercise 2

Now try something a little more complicated. This scale exercise uses the same notes as exercise 1, but there are bigger jumps between them.

Scales and exercises are a warm-up before you play a longer piece.

St Paul's Steeple

After playing the exercises, play a piece of music that includes many of the same notes. This will help reinforce what you have just practised.

Anon.

Showtime

Now that you have learnt all about playing
the recorder it's time for your performance!

La Morisque

At the end of this 16th-century piece you
will see the words "D.C. al Fine". This is a
performance direction that tells you to go
back to the beginning and play again until you
reach the word "Fine". Then you must stop.

Tempo di Minuetto

This piece was very popular in
the 18th century, when it was
frequently danced to.

James Hook

Gavotte

This piece is also a dance. It was
written by one of the most famous
composers of all time – Handel.

George Frideric Handel

Fingering chart

This handy chart shows you the finger and stave positions of all the notes covered in this book.

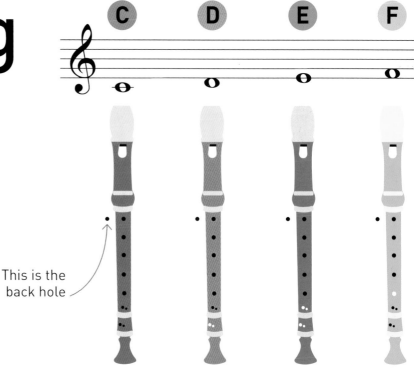

This is the back hole

Glossary

accidentals
Symbols such as sharps, flats, and naturals that change how high or low a note should be played

bar
Music is divided into bars. A time signature at the start of a piece tells you how many beats are in each bar

composer
Musician who writes a piece of music. Their name is usually written in the top-right corner of a piece

crotchet
Musical note worth one beat. It is written as a black circle with a stem

diaphragm
Muscle that moves up and down to control how much air is in your lungs

dotted note
A note with a dot next to it, which makes it half as long again. For example, a dotted minim lasts three beats

duet
Piece of music for two players to play together at the same time

dynamics
Special instructions that tell you when to play notes loudly or quietly

fingering
Covering up specific holes with your fingers in order to play different notes

flats
Symbols that tell you to play a note a little lower than normal, but higher than the next note down

key signature
Sharps or flats written next to the treble clef, indicating all notes of that type should be played sharp or flat

legato
Playing notes in a piece smoothly. Legato is the opposite of playing notes staccato

minim
Musical note worth two beats. It is written as a white circle with a stem

naturals
Symbols that cancel out the effects of any sharps or flats earlier in the bar

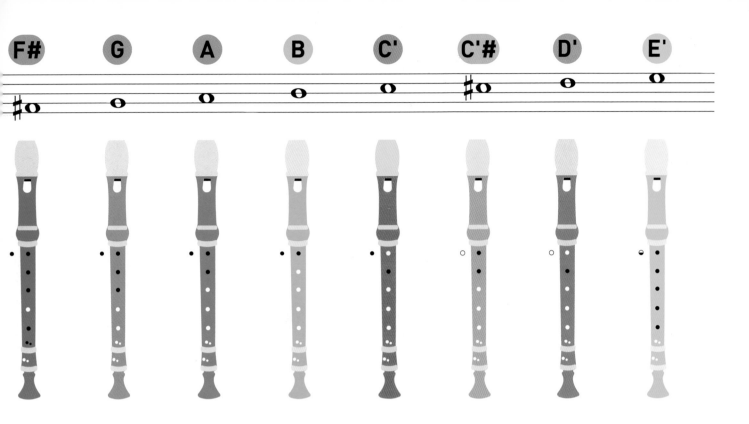

octave
Distance between two notes of the same letter. For example, the space between high D and low D

quaver
Musical note worth half a beat. It is written as a black circle with a tail on the stem

repeat sign
Two dots that indicate that the musician should play the section once more

rest
Silence in music. If you see a rest symbol, stop and count in silence for the length of the rest

scale
Series of eight notes, one after the other, getting higher or lower

semibreve
Musical note worth four beats. It is written as a white circle with no stem

sharps
Symbol that tells you to play a note a little higher than normal, but lower than the next note up

slurred notes
Two or more different notes joined together. Only the first note should be tongued

staccato notes
Short, punchy notes played with a quick movement of the tip of the tongue

stave
Music is written on a stave. It has five lines and four spaces

tied notes
Two or more of the same note joined together. Only the first note should be tongued

time signature
Two numbers next to a treble clef that show how many beats are in a bar, and what type of beats they are

tonguing
Technique of using your tongue to start each new note clearly

treble clef
Symbol that appears before the music at the start of a stave

Index

Acknowledgements

DORLING KINDERSLEY would like to thank: Jim Green for his design assistance; Olivia Stanford for her editorial assistance; Caroline Hunt for proofreading; and Helen Peters for the index.

All music, unless otherwise stated, courtesy of Lisete da Silva.

The publisher would like to thank the following for their kind permission to reproduce their photographs: (Key: a-above; b-below/bottom; c-centre; f-far; l-left; r-right; t-top)

5 Getty Images: Vincenzo Lombardo / Photographer's Choice RF (br). **8-9 Mollenhauer Recorders. 10 Corbis:** Wavebreak Media Ltd. / Alloy. **16 Dorling Kindersley:** Stephen Oliver (c). **18 Corbis:** Monalyn Gracia / Fancy.

Jacket images: *Back:* **Dreamstime.com:** Dimijana (tc).

All other images © Dorling Kindersley
For further information see: **www.dkimages.com**